Natural Disasters

Volcanoes

by
Allison Lassieur

Consultant:
John R. Reid, Ph.D.
Professor Emeritus of Geology
University of North Dakota

CAPSTONE BOOKS
an imprint of Capstone Press
Mankato, Minnesota

Capstone Books are published by Capstone Press
151 Good Counsel Drive, P.O. Box 669, Mankato, Minnesota 56002
http://www.capstone-press.com

Library of Congress Cataloging-in-Publication Data
Lassieur, Allison.
    Volcanoes/by Allison Lassieur.
    p. cm.—(Natural disasters)
    Includes bibliographical references and index.
    Summary: Examines the formation and eruption of volcanoes and describes the
damage they can cause.
    ISBN 0-7368-0589-3
    1. Volcanoes—Juvenile literature. [1. Volcanoes.] I. Title. II. Natural disasters
(Capstone Press)

QE521.3 .L394 2001
551.21—dc21   00-021415

Editorial Credits
Connie R. Colwell, editor; Timothy Halldin, cover designer and illustrator;
    Kia Bielke, illustrator; Heidi Schoof and Kimberly Danger, photo researchers

Photo Credits
Betty Crowell, 47
FPG International LLC/Andrea Sperling, 28; Ron Chapple, 43
Francis/Donna Caldwell/Pictor, 22
Gary Braasch, 6, 8, 41
Index Stock Imagery, cover; Index Stock Imagery/Tina Buckman, 38
International Stock/Phyllis Picardi, 4; Richard Hackett, 30; Douglas Peebles, 34
Kay Shaw, 36
Marv Binegar, 18
Reuters/Claro Cotes/Archive Photos, 32
Unicorn Stock Photos/Jeff Greenberg, 16, 26
Visuals Unlimited/Jay Pasachoff, 10; PallasPhoto Labs, Inc., 15; Doug Sokell, 20

1 2 3 4 5 6 06 05 04 03 02 01

Table of Contents

Chapter 1

Volcanoes

In the spring of 1980, strange things began to happen near Mount Saint Helens in Washington. This mountain is a volcano. Volcanoes have openings that allow ash, gases, and melted rock to erupt into the air.

Mount Saint Helens had last erupted more than 100 years before. But the volcano now had begun to rumble. A bulge the size of a football field formed on its side. Smoke and ash spat from the top of the mountain. Small earthquakes shook nearby areas.

Scientists visited Mount Saint Helens to watch for signs of an eruption. The scientists warned people who lived on or near Mount Saint Helens that the volcano might erupt

Mount Saint Helens erupted May 18, 1980.

The blast from Mount Saint Helens caused a great deal of damage to the surrounding land.

soon. Many of these people then left the area. But the warnings did not concern most people. No one knew when or if this eruption would occur. Many people continued to camp near Mount Saint Helens and nearby Spirit Lake.

Eruption

Mount Saint Helens erupted at 8:32 a.m. on May 18. The blast rattled windows throughout the area. A black cloud of ash rose a great distance into the air and darkened the sky. A hot wind rushed from the volcano and flattened entire forests. The plastic parts of nearby cars melted in the heat. The snow on top of the volcano melted. Rivers flooded and filled with mud, ash, trees, and dead animals.

The eruption was much larger than anyone had expected. Two scientists who were near the explosion jumped in a car to get away. They sped down dirt roads at nearly 100 miles (160 kilometers) per hour. The hot cloud of ash was right behind them. They were able to outrun the deadly blast.

Others were not so lucky. Scientist David Johnston was watching Mount Saint Helens from a ridge 5 miles (8 kilometers) away. When the volcano erupted, he shouted "This is it!" into a two-way radio. He was never heard from again. Another scientist had set up a camera to take pictures of the eruption. He died in his car as he tried to drive away. Many other people on Mount Saint Helens died. Some were never found.

Today, Mount Saint Helens is quiet. People can travel to a visitors' center near the volcano to see the eruption's damage. The area is

covered with black, dead trees. Spirit Lake is a muddy hole. Hills are gray, bare rocks. A few plants have started to grow. But it could be many years before normal life comes back to Mount Saint Helens.

Volcanoes

Volcanic eruptions are powerful natural forces. They can destroy life for miles or kilometers around. But these eruptions also help bring new plant life and soil to many areas.

Volcanoes are located throughout the world. Many of them are located in a band that circles the Pacific Ocean. Scientists call this area the "Ring of Fire." The Ring of Fire contains hundreds of volcanoes. But most of these volcanoes have not erupted for a long time.

Volcanic eruptions can destroy plant and animal life for miles or kilometers around.

Chapter 2

Why Volcanoes Erupt

Long ago, people did not know why volcanic eruptions occurred. These people often told stories to explain these natural disasters.

Volcano Legends

In ancient Rome, people believed that Vulcan was the blacksmith of the gods. Blacksmiths use heat to make and repair metal objects. The place where blacksmiths work is called a forge. Vulcan made weapons for Mars, the god of war. The Romans believed that volcanoes were the chimneys of Vulcan's forge. Hot melted rock and ash flowed out of a volcano when Vulcan made weapons. The word "volcano" comes from Vulcan's name.

The Romans believed that volcanoes were the chimneys of Vulcan's forge.

The ancient Greeks believed that the god Zeus used volcanoes as jails. Volcanic eruptions were the breath of giants as they tried to escape from the jails.

Earth's Crust

Today, scientists know more about why volcanic eruptions occur. Movements beneath Earth's crust create volcanoes. The crust is a rocky layer that covers Earth's entire surface.

It even covers the bottom of the oceans. The crust is between 5 and 25 miles (8 and 40 kilometers) thick. A thick layer of hot rock lies beneath the crust. This layer is called the mantle.

The crust and the upper mantle are broken into pieces like a cracked eggshell. The different pieces are called plates. There are about 10 large plates and 20 smaller plates. The plates sit on top of the mantle. Volcanoes form at the points where plates meet.

Parts of the mantle reach temperatures of 2,900 degrees Fahrenheit (1,600 degrees Celsius). These temperatures cause some of the rock to melt into a liquid. This liquid is called magma.

The mantle's heat causes the plates to move. Plates can move apart or bump into each other. This movement causes earthquakes. Plates that move apart tear the crust. The region where two plates move apart is called a rift zone. Most rift zones are located deep beneath the oceans.

One plate slides beneath another when plates bump into each other. The place where these plates meet is called a subduction zone.

Not all volcanoes form at the edges of plates. The Hawaiian Islands are some of the world's largest volcanoes. But they are not near plate edges. Scientists think a hot spot in Earth's crust formed these volcanoes. But they are not certain what causes these hot spots.

Eruptions

Rifts and cracks form openings in Earth's crust. Over time, magma pushes up through these openings.

Magma that reaches the surface of the Earth is called lava. Lava can be thin or thick depending on its temperature and composition. Hot, thin lava flows easily out of a volcano. Thicker lava cannot easily escape. Pressure builds up inside the volcano. The volcano then erupts with a huge blast. Hot ash, lava, and rocks burst from the volcano. Clouds of ash and rock can shoot miles or kilometers into the

Magma that reaches the surface of the Earth is called lava.

air. The ash cloud from one volcano can cover the entire Earth.

Types of Volcanoes

Scientists classify three types of volcanoes. These types are composite, shield, and cinder-cone volcanoes.

Composite volcanoes are tall and shaped like cones. These volcanoes are formed from piles of hardened lava, ash, and rocks.

Many composite volcanoes are thousands of feet or meters high. Some of the most well-known mountains in the world are composite volcanoes. These volcanoes include Mount Rainier in Washington and Mount Fuji in Japan. Composite volcano eruptions can be explosive or quiet.

Shield volcanoes form when lava flows. Lava flows in all directions from an opening in the top or side of the volcano. Lava hardens as it cools. The hardened lava builds up into a flat, broad mound. Some people think that this type of volcano looks like a warrior's shield.

Shield volcano eruptions created the Hawaiian Islands. Two Hawaiian shield volcanoes are the most active volcanoes in the world. These volcanoes are Kilauea and Mauna Loa. Kilauea has been erupting continuously since the 1980s.

Cinder-cone volcanoes look like small composite volcanoes. These volcanoes form when lava shoots from a vent into the air. The lava then hardens and falls as cinders. These

Cinder-cone volcanoes look like small composite volcanoes.

Crater Lake in Oregon was formed from the caldera of Mount Mazama.

rocks pile up around the volcano's vent. Cinder-cone volcanoes usually are less than 1,000 feet (300 meters) high. Their eruptions usually are quiet.

A volcano sometimes erupts with such force that it collapses and forms a caldera. These giant pits have steep, high walls. Some calderas fill with water and become lakes.

Crater Lake in Oregon was formed from Mount Mazama's caldera.

Classifications

Scientists classify volcanoes as active, dormant, or extinct. These classifications indicate how often volcanoes erupt.

An active volcano has erupted in the last 50 years. A dormant volcano has not erupted during the last 50 years. A volcano that has no historic record of erupting is considered extinct. But it still may erupt. A dormant volcano also can erupt at any time. Mount Saint Helens was a dormant volcano. Before May 18, 1980, it had not erupted for more than 100 years.

Chapter 3

The Power of an Eruption

Volcanic eruptions are one of the most powerful natural disasters. Their forces even can change weather conditions in other parts of the world.

Pyroclastic Flow

Many people think that lava is the most dangerous part of an eruption. But the deadliest part of a volcano is the pyroclastic flow. The pyroclastic flow also is called the volcanic hurricane. The pyroclastic flow is similar to strong wind storms called hurricanes. Hurricane winds can reach speeds

Volcanic eruptions are one of the most powerful natural disasters.

The force of a volcanic hurricane can blow down entire forests.

of 75 miles per hour (120 kilometers per hour) or more.

The pyroclastic flow may cause a huge blast of hot ash and cinder. The hot wind travels faster than most hurricane winds. It can be hundreds of degrees in temperature. The wind shoots tons of hot ash and rock at great speeds. The pyroclastic flow's force can blow down entire forests and destroy buildings. The forests at Mount Saint Helens were flattened by such a pyroclastic flow.

People who are caught in a pyroclastic flow die almost instantly. They suffocate when the hot ash clogs their throats. This wind can burn people's skin underneath their clothes. Volcano victims have been found with burns on their bodies. But their clothes are unharmed. Others die from being hit by flying rocks.

Other Forces

A volcano's ash can be almost as deadly as the pyroclastic flow. Ash can cover trees and plants and kill them. People and animals can choke on the ash and die. A huge ash cloud can remain in Earth's atmosphere. This cloud can prevent the sun's rays from reaching Earth's surface. This can cause temperatures to drop 1 to 2 degrees over Earth.

In 1815, a volcano called Mount Tambora erupted on the tiny Indonesian island of Sumbawa. Its ash cloud covered the entire Earth. Temperatures dropped. The cold weather

Volcanic Explosivity Index

VEI	Description	Frequency	Example
0	Non-Explosive	Daily	Kilauea
1	Gentle	Daily	Stromboli
2	Explosive	Weekly	Galeras, 1992
3	Severe	Yearly	Ruiz, 1985
4	Cataclysmic	Tens of Years	Galunggung, 1982
5	Paroxysmal	Hundreds of Years	Mount Saint Helens, 1981
6	Colossal	Hundreds of Years	Krakatau, 1983
7	Super-Colossal	Thousands of Years	Mount Tambora, 1815
8	Mega-Colossal	Ten-Thousands of Years	Yellowstone

and lack of sun killed crops in the United States. Many people starved. People called 1815 "the year without a summer."

Volcanoes also can cause deadly floods. The tops of many volcanoes are covered with snow throughout the year. Eruptions melt this snow and cause it to flood rivers and streams. The dirt, ash, and rocks from the eruption can make the rivers thick and muddy. This debris slows down the rivers' flow. These floods may destroy entire towns.

Lava flows kill few people. Lava usually moves very slowly. Most people have time to get out of its way.

But lava flows can be destructive. In Hawaii, lava flows have destroyed entire towns, a visitors' center, and a famous beach. A building or area covered with lava cannot be cleaned up. The lava hardens into rock as it cools. Anything that it covers is buried.

Scientists use the volcanic explosivity index (VEI) to measure the strength of volcanoes. Scientists rate volcanic eruptions with the numbers 0 through 8. Volcanoes rated 0 are usually weak and have thin lava. Volcanoes rated 8 have large amounts of ash and thick lava. These eruptions usually are more destructive.

Chapter 4

Famous Eruptions

Volcanic eruptions have claimed thousands of lives. Scientists study these eruptions to try to help predict other eruptions. This can help people prepare for volcanic eruptions.

Mount Vesuvius, Italy, A.D. 79

Nearly 2,000 years ago, the town of Pompeii was located in what is now Italy. This town was near a volcano called Mount Vesuvius. Earthquakes had shaken the town for years. But no eruptions had occurred.

On August 24, A.D. 79, Vesuvius erupted. Tons of rocks fell on the people of Pompeii. Gases and ash filled the air. Hundreds of people suffocated. Pompeii was buried in rock.

Mount Vesuvius is now a dormant volcano.

A man named Pliny the Elder tried to rescue people close to the mountain. But he suffocated before he could rescue anyone. His nephew Pliny the Younger wrote about the eruption. He was the first to describe what a volcanic eruption looked like.

In 1738, a man digging a ditch found Pompeii. This man also found the forms of people who had been buried in Pompeii's ash and rock. The people's bodies had decayed. But their forms had been preserved in hardened mud. People later made plaster casts of these forms.

Today, much of Pompeii has been uncovered. Tourists can visit the shops and homes of people who once lived there. They also can visit Vesuvius. It is now dormant. But it still could erupt again.

Mount Tambora, Indonesia, 1815

Mount Tambora erupted for the first time on April 15, 1815. Villagers on nearby islands heard loud explosions. A light rain of ash then

Today, much of Pompeii has been uncovered.

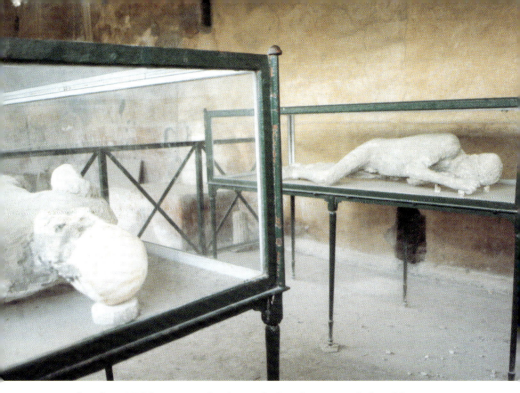

In the 1700s, people found the forms of the Mount Vesuvius eruption's victims.

began to fall. The volcano erupted for three months. People could hear the explosions 1,000 miles (1,600 kilometers) away. The ash cloud blocked the sun's rays in places as far as 300 miles (483 kilometers) away. People had to light candles to see during the day. Rocks blew out of the volcano's top. A pyroclastic flow blew down houses, tore up trees, and lifted people and animals into the air. The sea rose and flooded farms. About 10,000 people died during the eruption. More than 82,000 people later died of starvation and disease caused by the eruption's effects.

North America is more than 10,000 miles (16,000 kilometers) from Indonesia. But North America experienced unusual weather caused by the volcanic ash. Snow fell in June. Frost killed crops in August. North Americans called that year "eighteen hundred and froze to death." But these people did not know that a volcano had caused this weather.

Mount Pinatubo, the Philippines, 1991

The eruption of Mount Pinatubo in the Philippines was one of the largest of the last 100 years. On April 2, 1991, steam burst out of the volcano's top. More than 200 earthquakes shook the area in one day. Gases filled the air. Ash covered the land near the volcano. Most people did not expect this eruption. But scientists had warned people about the eruption. About 200,000 people left their homes in time to avoid injury.

Scientists watched Mount Pinatubo for weeks after the eruption. They again warned people to leave the area. On June 15, the volcano's noises became louder. An explosion blew off the volcano's top.

Pyroclastic flows destroyed forests. So many earthquakes occurred that the machines used to measure them broke down. The sky turned dark with ash and dirt. Ash mixed with rain and collapsed roofs.

Mount Pinatubo erupted for five years. Today, it is inactive. But it still is not safe to live in the area. Rain mixes with loose ash and causes large mudflows each year.

The eruption of Mount Pinatubo was one of the largest of the last 100 years.

Chapter 5

Surviving an Eruption

Volcanic eruptions are difficult to predict. Some volcanoes erupt slowly for dozens of years. Others explode violently with little warning. Some spit out steam and ash but do not erupt. Others erupt for years and then stop suddenly.

Scientists study volcanoes to learn how to predict them. They take pictures and videos. They measure volcanoes' actions. They sometimes take samples of lava. The information they gather can help predict future eruptions.

Scientists study volcanoes in order to learn how to predict them.

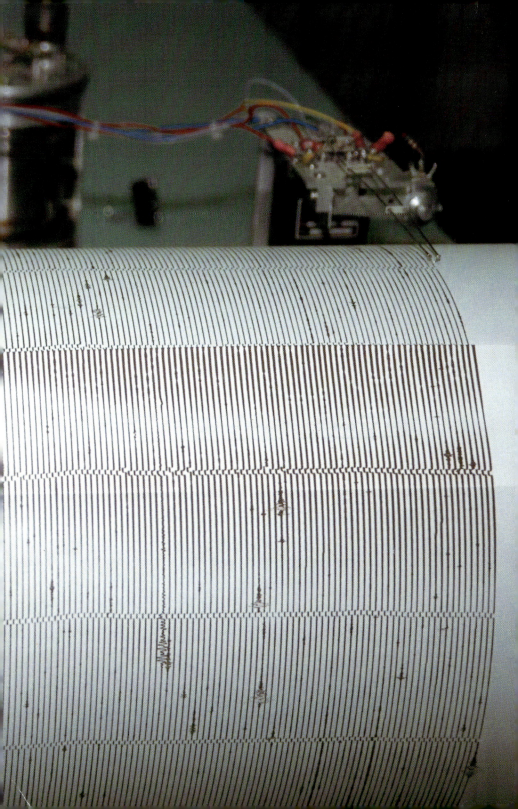

Predictions

Scientists use instruments to try to predict when volcanoes will erupt. These instruments are called seismometers and tiltmeters. Both instruments react to the magma inside the volcano. Magma that changes or moves is a sign that a volcano may erupt.

Earthquakes are signs that a volcano may erupt. Earthquakes always occur with volcanic eruptions. Scientists use special instruments called seismometers to help detect earthquakes. These instruments may indicate that a volcano will erupt.

Scientists issue warnings if a volcano shows signs of erupting. They tell people living near the volcano to leave the area. Government workers often put up roadblocks to keep people from entering the area once the residents have left.

Warning Scale

Scientists use a number scale to indicate the danger of a possible eruption. This scale

Seismometers may indicate that a volcano will erupt.

helps people know how dangerous a volcano warning is.

The numbers of the scale range from 0 to 5. A rating of 0 indicates that there will be no eruption in the immediate future. A rating of 1 indicates that no eruption is likely any time soon. A rating of 2 indicates that an eruption could happen. Small earthquakes may occur during ratings of 1 and 2. Some lava also may be visible. A rating of 3 indicates that an eruption may occur within two weeks. Many earthquakes may occur. The volcano also may release gases and steam. A rating of 4 indicates that an eruption is possible within 24 hours. Large earthquakes may occur. A rating of 5 indicates that an eruption is in progress.

Living with Volcanoes

Scientists cannot accurately predict volcanic eruptions. People in some areas of the world must live with occasional volcanic eruptions.

In the past, people have taken unusual actions to avoid damage and injury from

People in some areas of the world must learn to live with occasional volcanic eruptions.

volcanic eruptions. In Hawaii, people built walls to keep lava flows from destroying land and buildings. In Iceland, people sprayed cold water on lava to try to stop it from flowing. In Sicily, people tried to stop lava by blasting underground tunnels to redirect the flow.

Volcanic eruptions are powerful forces that can destroy a great deal of land and life. It often takes decades before the land recovers from a volcanic eruption. But eruptions also help form new land and rich soil. Volcanic eruptions are important parts of nature.

Volcanic eruptions help form new land and rich soil.

Words To Know

crust (KRUHST)—the thin outer layer of Earth's surface

eruption (i-RUHPT-shuhn)—the action of throwing out rock, hot ash, and lava with great force

lava (LAH-va)—hot, melted rock that flows from a volcano

magma (MAG-muh)—melted rock deep beneath Earth's surface

plate (PLAYT)—a section of Earth's crust

rift (RIFT)—a tear or break in Earth's crust

suffocate (SUHF-uh-kate)—to kill by stopping oxygen to the lungs

vent (VENT)—the opening in a volcano

To Learn More

Arnold, Nick. *Volcano, Earthquake, and Hurricane.* Austin, Texas: Raintree Steck-Vaughn, 1997.

Griffey, Harriet. *Volcanoes: and Other Natural Disasters.* New York: D K Publishing, 1998.

Lampton, Christopher. *Volcano.* A Disaster! Book. Brookfield, Conn.: Millbrook Press, 1991.

Sands, Stella. *Exploring Natural Disasters.* Eyes on Adventure. Chicago: Kidsbooks, 1996.

Useful Addresses

Capulin Volcano National Monument
P.O. Box 40
Capulin, NM 88414

Crater Lake National Park
P.O. Box 7
Crater Lake, OR 97604

Hawaii Volcanoes National Park
P.O. Box 52
Hawaii National Park, HI 96718

**Mount Saint Helens National Volcanic
    Monument**
Route One
P.O. Box 369
Amboy, WA 98601

Internet Sites

National Park Service
http://www.nps.gov

USGS Cascades Volcano Observatory
http://vulcan.wr.usgs.gov

USGS Volcanoes
http://pubs.usgs.gov/gip/volc/cover2.html

Volcanoes Online
http://library.advanced.org/17457/english.html

Volcano World
http://volcano.und.nodak.edu/vw.html

Index